in
the
news™

SAME-SEX MARRIAGE

THE DEBATE

Jeanne Nagle

ROSEN
PUBLISHING®

New York

For couples everywhere who fall in love and
wish to devote their lives to each other

Published in 2010 by The Rosen Publishing Group, Inc.
29 East 21st Street, New York, NY 10010

Copyright © 2010 by The Rosen Publishing Group, Inc.

First Edition

Library of Congress Cataloging-in-Publication Data

Nagle, Jeanne.
Same-sex marriage: the debate / Jeanne Nagle.
     p. cm.—(In the news)
Includes bibliographical references and index.
ISBN 978-1-4358-3582-5 (library binding)
ISBN 978-1-4358-8546-2 (pbk)
ISBN 978-1-4358-8547-9 (6 pack)
1. Same-sex marriage—United States. 2. Same-sex marriage—Law and legislation—United States. 3. Gay rights—United States. I. Title.
HQ1034.U5N34 2010
306.84'80973—dc22

                                                                    2009019653

Manufactured in Malaysia

CPSIA Compliance Information: Batch #TWW10YA: For Further Information contact Rosen Publishing, New York, New York at 1-800-237-9932

On the cover: Clockwise from upper left: Many same-sex couples are taking advantage of laws that allow them to marry in some states; wedding cake toppers are undergoing a change worldwide, as are preconceived notions of what marriage is; protestors, both for and against, are becoming a more common sight in the United States as the debate surrounding same-sex marriage continues.

contents

Same-Sex Marriage in the News

For years, the only time weddings were considered newsworthy was when celebrities, royalty, or the rich tied the knot. That situation changed as the twenty-first century rolled around. Suddenly, ordinary people getting married started making headlines left and right. The media (television, radio, newspapers, magazines, and the Internet) were filled with stories of everyday couples in love who wanted to marry.

So what is behind the increased interest in weddings and matrimony? At the root of all the media attention is a very public and heated debate about who should be allowed to get married. Some people believe that marriage can only exist between a man and a woman. Others think that everyone should have the right to marry. That includes gay men and lesbians, who are romantically and sexually attracted to members of the same sex. A marriage between two men or two women is called a same-sex marriage.

Once-private wedding ceremonies have become media events now that same-sex couples are fighting for and, in some cases, winning the right to marry.

Where the Situation Stands

According to the most recent federal census, there are around 777,000 same-sex couples living in the United States, residing in every state in the country. (That number may rise when the next U.S. Census is conducted in 2010.) Only six states allow these couples to legally marry.

States decide for themselves whether or not to let same-sex couples get married. As of 2009, six states

(Massachusetts, Connecticut, Iowa, Vermont, and Maine) allow same-sex marriage; twenty-nine states have a constitutional amendment prohibiting same-sex marriage. Three states allow civil unions for same-sex couples, and five states, plus the District of Columbia, allow same-sex domestic partnerships. These are legal agreements designed to recognize the commitment of gay couples under the law. Civil unions and domestic partnerships do not offer many of the legal and social advantages of marriage, however. Also, states don't have to acknowledge that a gay couple is married under the laws of another state. In fact, only New York and the District of Columbia have acted to honor and recognize same-sex marriages from another state.

Canadian provinces and territories used to have the right to determine the legality of same-sex marriage. Then in 2005, the Canadian Parliament passed the Civil Marriage Act, which made same-sex marriage legal nationwide. Canada is one of six nations that permit gay couples across the country to marry. The United States, on the other hand, has the Defense of Marriage Act (DOMA). Passed by the U.S. Congress in 1996, the act bars the federal government from recognizing, or accepting, same-sex marriages and allows states to do the same. Only heterosexual marriages, or marriages between a man and a woman, count in the eyes of the U.S. government.

All residents of a state or country are affected by legislation for or against same-sex marriage. Consequently, people raise their voices in public forums to let their concerns be heard.

Why Same-Sex Marriage Gets News Coverage

Same-sex marriage tends to upset the status quo, meaning an established way of life. What makes a marriage in most cultures has been established for a long time. Men and women have been marrying each other for as long as anyone can remember. Two men or two women have not. Therefore, the idea of gay men and lesbians marrying creates controversy. A controversy is an event or concept about which people have differing opinions.

Expressing these opinions often leads to conflict. As you may have learned in English class, conflict and tension are the basis of good storytelling. They give people something to root for or against and get them involved in the action. The news media are in the business of selling real-life stories, for information and entertainment. Conflict makes stories juicier, which draws more and more people into the action of local and world events.

For better or worse, controversy is big business for the news media. When people are interested in a subject, they want to read or hear more about it. Controversial subjects are of interest to a great number of people. That translates into climbing newspaper and magazine sales, and larger television and radio audiences.

Areas of Controversy

Getting married is an intensely personal and private decision. Being married, on the other hand, turns out to be more of a public matter. Marriage has legal, social, and religious elements attached to it, and married couples enjoy certain benefits in the eyes of the law, religious institutions, and society as a whole. Changing the commonly accepted definition of marriage often challenges existing laws and religious traditions.

On the legal front, married couples have more rights granted to them. For instance, spouses can file their taxes jointly, which usually saves them money. The right to benefits in the United States, particularly those given by the federal government, is another problematic legal issue. These include health benefits, wage and worker compensation benefits, and Social Security or pension benefits. Currently, there are more than 1,100 laws that make certain rights and benefits in the United States available to married couples only.

Same-sex couples would have to be legally married in order to be eligible for these benefits. However, the federal government does not recognize same-sex marriages as being legal. Even if a gay couple is married in a state or country that allows same-sex marriage, they still aren't considered married by the U.S. government.

Religion is another area of controversy. Many world religions refuse to accept the idea of same-sex marriage. Religious and spiritual leaders typically object to gays marrying on what they believe are moral grounds. Basically, morality is the ability to tell the difference between right and wrong, and choosing to do the right thing. Various religions base what they believe to be right and wrong on their scriptures, which are sacred writings. For example, Christians use the Bible, Jews the

Torah, and Muslims the Qu'ran. Each of these texts has passages that religious leaders say forbid homosexuality, which is love for and attraction to the same sex.

Society as a whole also recognizes the benefits of marriage, particularly when there are children involved. While a recent report from the Centers for Disease Control and Prevention (CDC) shows that 40 percent of births in the United States in 2007 were to single or unmarried women, overall, American society views a two-parent household with children as the ideal.

A Timely and Timeless Issue

The debate over same-sex marriage has been around for years. One of the top priorities of the gay rights movement, which became an organized cause in the United States during the 1960s, is marriage. Other priorities of the gay rights movement include fighting workplace discrimination and hate crimes, as well as securing the right to serve in the military and adopt children or be a foster parent. The battle over same-sex marriage seems to gather strength and make more headlines during political elections, especially in the United States. Election years are the perfect time to push for laws that either make same-sex marriage legal or ban it.

This strategy was very apparent during U.S. elections in 2004, 2006, and 2008. Many states tried to pass amendments, or legal additions, to their constitutions. A constitution is a written document outlining the organization, authority, and laws of a government. Each state has its own constitution, which applies to citizens of that state, in addition to the U.S. Constitution, which applies to all Americans. In each election year mentioned, opponents of same-sex marriage worked to get enough votes to pass amendments that would outlaw same-sex marriage. Some passed, while others did not.

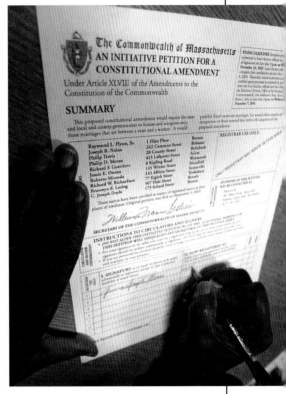

Enough signatures from concerned citizens can put a proposition to change a state's constitution on the ballot so people can vote on the idea.

Either way, the move brought same-sex marriage into the national spotlight each and every time.

But the question of whether or not same-sex couples should be allowed to marry is more than just a political concern every couple of years. The right of every person to be treated in a fair and equal manner is an issue that never goes out of style. In the United States, various groups have fought for equal rights. For instance, women rallied for the right to vote, which they earned in 1920. Decades later, they pushed for a greater measure of fairness at work through what was known as the women's liberation movement. "Liberation" is another word for "freedom." The civil rights movement of the 1960s came about as a way to end discrimination against and obtain equal rights for African Americans.

Today, many who support gay rights see their movement as being a lot like the civil rights movement. Gay people feel as if they are in a battle to gain the same rights given freely to heterosexuals, including the right to marry.

What's at Stake

Same-sex marriage is an issue that is likely to have an impact on more than just the gay population. Beyond equal rights for same-sex couples, there are also implications for heterosexual unmarried couples. Laws and rules that deny certain rights based on marital status cannot make exceptions for couples who are not gay. For instance, under the law, heterosexual couples who choose not to marry are out of luck when it comes to a large number of federal privileges and benefits, just like same-sex couples.

There are also questions about who ultimately has the power to make decisions about what marriage is and isn't. Does the government determine the definition of marriage through the laws it passes? Do courts get to choose, on a case-by-case basis, which people have the right to get married? How much influence should religious institutions have on the matter? The role of each of these institutions has yet to be settled completely.

Governmental involvement can be broken down even further. The Tenth Amendment to the U.S. Constitution gives individual states control over matters that are not prohibited to them by the Constitution or specifically granted to the federal government. So far, same-sex marriage has been handled by the states. Yet by not recognizing, or acknowledging, same-sex marriage at all, the federal government has been accused of overruling the states' rights to make such marriages legal. In this way, same-sex marriage could be a testing ground for the balance of power between states and the federal government.

The Evolution of Marriage

2

While the history of marriage is very complex and differs depending on what culture, country, and time period you are studying, in the broadest sense, marriage is, and has been, a union between two people that is recognized by law. What has changed throughout time are the particulars, meaning the details.

A society's customs and practices usually reflect what is going on during a given period of time. Naturally, as the times change, so do the customs. As an example, think about the different means of communication through the ages. Hundreds of years ago, people could get messages to each other only by writing letters or speaking in person. The invention of the telegraph machine and the telephone made communication easier and faster. In modern times, electronic devices have made texting and e-mail the favorite ways to keep in touch and share information. Each advance in technology has changed the communication practices of entire societies.

Customs associated with marriage have also adapted to the times. For instance, brides used to enter into marriage with a dowry, a gift of money and goods a woman's family gave to the groom. The gift had been meant, in part, to help the couple set up their household. Dowries went out of fashion in most parts of the world during the 1800s. Today, that tradition has been replaced by the practice of bridal showers, where gifts are given to help the couple start their new life together.

As customs have changed, so have various cultures' definitions of what it means to be married. This change has not always sat well with the public. Same-sex marriage is viewed by some to be an unacceptable change from the more traditional "one man and one woman" view of marriage. So is same-sex marriage a threat or merely another in a long line of changes? A quick look at the history of marriage, and the challenges the institution has faced, can help put discussions of same-sex marriage into perspective.

The Law of the Land

In the beginning, marriage wasn't so much about love between two partners as it was about making sure people didn't become extinct. One of the biggest reasons for two people to get married in ancient times was so that they would have children. Many believed they had a

In the Middle Ages, noblemen and noblewomen produced several offspring as a way to keep the family name going through the ages, as this painting of a German prince and his family depicts.

sacred duty to populate the earth, or supply the world with human beings. Others believed that creating more people made their country or tribe stronger. Having a large family also ensured that the family name and DNA would live on. Through their descendants, people felt like they would never be forgotten.

In ancient Rome, there was a period of time when the number of marriages was declining and many married couples were choosing not to have children. Worried that there wouldn't be enough upper-class citizens around to keep the Roman Empire powerful, Emperor Augustus (63 BCE–14 CE) created laws that encouraged marriage and birth. The effect was that people were penalized for not marrying. Single men could not hold positions of authority, and adults without spouses were taxed more heavily than married couples.

Of course, then as now, sex was required to have babies, not marriage. But without marriage, a father was not obligated to provide for his children or their mother. Also, children born outside of marriage did not have certain rights. Illegitimate, or out-of-wedlock, children could not inherit their father's property or wealth.

The Business End of Marriage

There was a financial element to most early marriages as well. While the bride's family was expected to provide a dowry, the groom generally paid a bride price. A man would give a small sum of money or parcel of land to the bride's father as a way of showing that he was serious about the marriage. Men did not buy women with a bride price. Their gift was more about compensation for the loss of a woman's ability to work and bear children for her own family.

So important was a woman's worth to her husband's family that some cultures had a custom in place that protected a wife as a valuable asset. Levirate was the

A bride price is not made up of only money, but also jewels and other precious objects. A formal presentation of gifts is usually part of the tradition in many countries.

practice of a widow marrying her husband's brother after her husband had died. Usually, levirate occurred when the woman and her first husband had no children. Marrying the man's brother and having children with him made sure that the bloodlines of the two families remained intact. It also protected the investment the families had made in each other through the dowry and bride price.

In the Middle Ages, upper-class couples had to sign marriage contracts, which specified who got what as far as land and other material wealth were concerned. These contracts were a record of what the bride and groom, and their families, were bringing to the marriage. In some cultures, contracts also spelled out what spouses expected of each other. For instance, a condition could be added that the husband never leave his wife.

Money and land weren't the only considerations. Some marriages in the past were designed for security and power. In the Middle Ages, nobility—meaning kings, queens, other royalty, and members of the ruling class—frequently married to build alliances. Nations joined by the marriage of their rulers could be reasonably sure that fighting would not break out between them. Also, they counted on allied countries to take their side in disputes and wars with other nations.

Many of these marriages were arranged affairs. In an arranged marriage, parents find a spouse for their child in a way that's kind of like a business agreement. In extreme cases, a couple may meet only once before their wedding. Although they're not as common as in the past, arranged marriages still occur in certain parts of the world, such as India and the Middle East.

Enter the Church

For a long time, marriage was considered a private matter. Couples didn't need the approval of either the government or a religious institution to be considered married. Exchanging private vows and living together as a married couple were often all that were necessary for a marriage to exist. Clergymen might be asked to say a blessing over the union, but that was the only way religion was involved.

That situation changed as the Protestant and Roman Catholic churches began to take a greater role in wedding ceremonies. The Council of Trent, which was a series of meetings of Roman Catholic theologians to reorganize church guidelines and which opened in Italy in 1545 and closed there in 1563, declared marriage a sacrament. A sacrament is a holy rite that is supposed to bring a person closer to God. From then on, faithful Catholics would be considered married only if they had a public ceremony overseen by a priest, with at least two witnesses present. Protestants had the Marriage Ordinance in Geneva (Switzerland), which was created by John Calvin and other pastors around the same time and had similar requirements.

Religious involvement made marriage a more formal affair, with plenty of rules, rituals, and restrictions. Eventually, civil marriages, which are under the control of governments, became more popular throughout most of the Western world. Even so, many couples still sought religious ceremonies and the blessing of their church.

Past and Present Challenges to Traditional Marriage

The choice to have a civil or religious ceremony remains to this day—at least for couples who want what has become known as a "traditional" wedding. A union between one man and one woman is the most common type of marriage, so it is referred to as being traditional.

In 1967, Mildred and Richard Loving were the first to win a court challenge against Virginia's state law banning interracial marriage. Their victory signaled a change in how Americans viewed marriage.

Over the years, traditional marriage has been put to the test several times, and its boundaries have been pushed.

One such challenge has come from the practice of plural marriages. Polygamy, or having more than one spouse at a time, is the most well-known form of plural marriage. Technically, one man having more than one wife is polygyny, and one woman having several husbands is polyandry. The Bible features several prominent figures, including Abraham and King David, with multiple wives.

Therefore, it is assumed that the practice of plural marriages has been around at least since biblical times.

These days, polygamy is illegal just about everywhere in the world. However, there are still certain groups that allow plural marriages, typically under the protection of religious freedom. In the United States, members of the Mormon faith engaged in polygamy until the Church of Jesus Christ of Latter-day Saints, also known as the Mormon Church, officially stopped the practice in 1890. Still, some sects, or groups that have broken away from the main church, practice polygamy today. Islam, which is the Muslim faith, permits polygamy but doesn't encourage the practice. Any Muslim wishing to have a plural marriage must follow strict legal requirements. In many Muslim nations and cultures, polygamy is very rare or even nonexistent.

More recent challenges to traditional marriage concern who gets married instead of how many. Up until the 1960s, marriage between a man and a woman of different races was against the law in the United States. Under the law, couples with different religions may not marry in Israel, and they find it hard to be wed in Malaysia and other Muslim countries. Elsewhere in the world, interfaith marriage is legally allowed but may be forbidden by a person's house of worship. And, of course, there is the most recent challenge to traditional unions, same-sex marriage.

Types of Unions and Their Benefits

Mention that you are married and just about everyone on the planet will understand what you mean. No matter what language is being spoken or the particular word a culture uses, marriage is a universally understood concept. It is recognized all around the world as a legal, loving commitment between people.

Marriage is different from all other types of relationships and cannot be duplicated. Still, many countries, and virtually all of the American states, have tried to create alternative versions of marriage for gay people. Civil unions and domestic partnerships are legal agreements designed to recognize the commitment of gay couples under the law. In Europe, these relationships may be called registered partnerships or life partnerships.

Being in a civil union or domestic partnership entitles a couple to certain rights and benefits that single people do not have. However, neither of these types of relationships offers as many advantages and perks as marriage.

Definitions and Current Status of Same-Sex Unions

Civil unions are a lot like civil marriages. The term "civil" in this case means legal, not religious. Civil unions are ways for governments to acknowledge that a gay couple has declared they will love and take care of each other, making them legally responsible for each other. In the United States, whether or not to offer civil unions is a matter for individual states to decide.

Domestic partnerships are for people who live together as if they are married, but they are neither married nor joined by a civil union. Both same-sex and opposite-sex couples can register as domestic partners. Typically, more same-sex couples register as domestic partners than heterosexual couples. As with civil unions, there is no involvement by the federal government. Domestic partnerships are registered at the state level, as each state sees fit.

Legal unions for gay couples are relatively new. A 2005 report by BBC News says that Denmark was the first country to pass laws acknowledging the rights of registered same-sex couples, in 1989. A few other Scandinavian countries and France followed Denmark's lead throughout the 1990s. Germany has given limited rights to gay couples since 2001.

A Vermont couple celebrates the state's decision to legally recognize same-sex unions by registering with their town clerk. In 2000, Vermont became the first U.S. state to offer civil unions.

In the United States, Vermont has the honor of being the first state to offer civil unions, starting in 2000. The decision to offer civil unions came about after the Vermont Supreme Court ruled that the state could not refuse to give gay couples the same legal protection it gave heterosexual couples. Vermont was faced with a decision: Either legalize same-sex marriage in the state, or offer gay couples partnership status that was equal to that of marriage. When the state chose the latter, civil unions had arrived in the United States.

New Jersey's civil union law went into effect in February 2007. New Hampshire's law allowing civil unions went into effect on January 1, 2008. Five states (Oregon, Hawaii, Maine, Washington, and California) and the District of Columbia have domestic partnership laws. In addition, Maryland provides certain benefits to domestic partners.

How Civil Unions and Domestic Partnerships Work

To enter into a civil union in the United States, two people of the same sex go through a procedure similar to what a man and a woman go through to have a civil marriage ceremony. First, both parties have to be at least eighteen years old. Then they have to get a license from the state.

Within a certain number of days from when the license is issued, the same-sex couple needs to have an official certify their union. Judges, town clerks, and justices of the peace are qualified to certify civil unions. The blessing of a member of the clergy also counts as certification. But because not many religions recognize civil unions, their clergy do not usually take part in this type of ceremony.

As with civil unions, those who enter a domestic partnership must be at least eighteen years old. People in this type of arrangement must prove that they live in the same home and share living expenses. They must also be willing to be legally responsible for their partner. Instead of a license, domestic partners sign a legal declaration, which is a type of contract.

Benefits

Gay couples are entitled to several state benefits once they enter into a civil union or a domestic partnership. Benefits are advantages given to certain groups of people, usually involving money. Companies helping to pay for health care and contributing to retirement savings accounts are common benefits.

As legally binding agreements, domestic partnerships require a signed declaration in order to be valid. A certificate takes the place of a marriage license in such arrangements.

The advantages given to legally joined couples revolve around such matters as tax exemptions, property rights, and the ability to make legal and medical decisions for a partner who is unable to do so for himself or herself. Adoption and child custody, inheritance, and protection against discrimination based on marital status may also

Same-sex couples not only want the right to marry, but also access to the same federal benefits and rights as married heterosexual couples.

be covered, depending on where the union or partnership takes place. Couples in a civil union or domestic partnership can add specific benefits to their relationship agreement through an individually prepared prenuptial contract, just like married couples.

Benefits gained after entering into a civil union or domestic partnership vary greatly from state to state. For instance, couples in a Vermont civil union receive benefits that are practically equal to what married couples within the state get. Those in domestic partnerships in Washington State only get power of attorney, inheritance rights, and hospital visitation privileges. In general, it is safe to say that civil unions offer more statewide benefits than domestic partnerships.

Not Quite Marriage Material

At first glance, it seems as if civil unions and marriage are pretty equal. By law, civil unions are set up to provide the same state benefits that are offered to married couples. There's something missing from the equality picture, however. The benefits given to married heterosexual couples apply no matter where they choose to live or visit. The rights given under civil unions and domestic partnerships are legal only in the state where the relationship began.

Also, neither civil unions nor domestic partnerships offer U.S. federal benefits, which legally married couples in every state receive as soon as they say "I do." The U.S. Government Accountability Office (GAO) lists more than a thousand benefits available to married couples only. For instance, benefit payments from federal programs like Social Security or Medicare automatically go to the surviving wife or husband when a working spouse dies. People in civil unions and domestic partnerships do not qualify for such benefits. Although they are a legal couple in their state, they are not married and not legally together in the eyes of the federal government.

Arguments for and Against Same-Sex Marriage

Polls recently conducted in the United States reveal just how divided the nation is on the subject of same-sex marriage. A 2008 CNN/Opinion Research Corporation poll indicates a fairly even split between those who support same-sex marriage and those who oppose it. (Those who are against gay people marrying have a slight majority.) The most recent CBS News/*New York Times* poll comes to the same conclusion. A Field Poll taken in California, a state that is at the center of the same-sex marriage debate, shows the narrowest margin between support and opposition. Forty-eight percent of survey participants would like to see same-sex marriage become legal in California, while 47 percent are opposed. The remaining 5 percent are undecided.

Interestingly, these polls also provide a clue as to how specific groups of people feel about the matter. For instance, younger people (ages eighteen to thirty) are more likely to support same-sex marriage, while older people (over age sixty-five) are against it. People who regularly attend religious services generally do not favor same-sex couples marrying. Those who say they aren't very religious are more likely to approve of gay couples having the right to marry. People who identify themselves as Democrats or liberals are in favor of making same-sex marriage legal. Republicans and conservatives are more likely to oppose it.

What this all means is that there are very strong arguments on both sides of the same-sex marriage debate. As hinted at in recent polls, religious and political beliefs play a role in forming arguments both pro and con.

Discrimination and Equality

On the pro side, people say that banning same-sex marriage is not only unfair, but it is also discriminatory. Denying people basic rights based on their class, religion, race, or sexual orientation is discrimination, and it is illegal. People who support gay rights believe that marriage is a basic human right. Following that logic, not allowing two men or two women to get married is a form of illegal discrimination.

Civil unions are also a form of discrimination, say some gay rights activists. As an opinion piece in the April 1, 2007, *New York Times* declares, civil unions can be seen as "little more than . . . a second-class form of matrimony." In other words, civil unions may have been

Giving same-sex couples benefits that are similar to those offered to married couples but still treating them as a separate group is not the same as equality, argue gay rights activists.

created as a way to calm down gay couples by providing similar benefits and protections without actually having to give them the right to marry. This is a concept known as "separate but equal."

The argument against "separate but equal" is that the very act of separating one class of people from another implies that the second class isn't considered as good as the first. After all, if they were as good, why not just give them the same facilities, benefits, etc., right off the bat?

Opposition on Religious Grounds

The strongest opposition to same-sex marriage comes from religious groups. Their belief is that marriage is a sacred union between one man and one woman only. Many who are against same-sex marriage hold the idea that marriage is for procreation, or having babies. The argument goes that because two people of the same sex can't have children naturally with each other, they shouldn't be married.

Complicating the discussion further is the fact that almost all religions believe that homosexuality itself is a sin. The idea is that gays should not even be practicing a same-sex lifestyle, let alone be allowed to take part in a special sacrament like marriage. Religious groups frequently use the Bible and other religious texts to prove that their view of homosexuality is correct. As a December 2008 *Newsweek* cover story on religion and same-sex marriage notes, several passages in the Bible seem to discourage sex between two men, calling the act an "abomination."

However, as the *Newsweek* article points out, the Bible also gives examples of love and marriage that fall outside the traditional mold. There are many references to polygamy and people marrying outside their faith, which was also forbidden at the time. Beyond that, those who support same-sex marriage believe that the

Using religious texts as their guide and inspiration, some people believe that a divine plan for marriage is being ignored when same-sex couples are allowed to marry.

New Testament's general message to love each other regardless of differences is an additional argument in favor of same-sex unions.

Finally, many people believe that using the Bible or other religious texts to support a ban on same-sex marriage is unfair because of the long history in the United States of separation of church and state. This means that the job of the government should not be influenced by, and should be kept separate from, the practices and beliefs of religious organizations.

Preserving the Institution of Marriage

Another argument is that legalizing same-sex unions will ruin marriage and make it meaningless. The thinking is that marriage is special because it is unlike any other relationship. Opponents fear that allowing same-sex marriage is a "slippery slope," meaning a situation that starts a bad chain of events. Their concern is that changing the definition of marriage to include gay couples opens the door to legalizing all sorts of other "nontraditional" marriages, such as polygamy. Eventually, marriage would mean so many different things that it would lose its special quality and no longer matter.

What would happen next is obvious to those who don't want the meaning of marriage to change. Marriage is crucial to creating healthy families. Stable family life helps keep human societies strong. If marriage doesn't matter, people won't feel the need to get married, and families will suffer.

Supporters of same-sex marriage generally agree that stable families are important. However, they disagree that legalizing same-sex unions would weaken marriage. They believe that the opposite is true. Allowing gay couples to legally marry could actually create more happy families. Also, by choosing to get married, couples of all sexual orientations show that they value marriage, which makes married life more appealing to future generations.

The more couples that are married, no matter their sexual orientation, the stronger the institution becomes.

Constitutional Interpretations

During the 1967 U.S. Supreme Court case that made interracial marriage legal (*Loving v. Virginia*), Chief Justice Earl Warren quoted one of the most famous lines from the Declaration of Independence. He wrote that the freedom to marry was essential to each American's "pursuit of happiness." Today's discussion of same-sex marriage has people referencing another historic American document. Both sides of the same-sex marriage debate can point to the U.S. Constitution to back up their claims.

The First Amendment to the Constitution makes freedom of religion an undeniable right. Religious leaders are concerned that legalizing same-sex marriage will force congregations to take part in a ceremony that goes against their beliefs, as well as their constitutional right to practice those beliefs.

The First Amendment also makes it clear that the government should not make laws based on religious beliefs. In other words, the First Amendment legally separates church and state matters. Keep in mind that marriage is both a religious and a civil (state) matter. Based on freedom of religion, religious institutions have

Depending on a person's opinion, the ability of same-sex couples to marry and raise children would either strengthen or harm the institution of marriage.

the right not to perform same-sex marriage ceremonies because of their beliefs. However, those who are for same-sex marriage argue that—thanks again to the First Amendment—houses of worship do not have the right to deny gay couples the right to a civil, or state-authorized, marriage.

Another argument has been made that banning same-sex marriage violates, or goes against, the Fourteenth Amendment to the U.S. Constitution. Basically, this amendment guarantees equal protection to all Americans. Gay rights supporters claim that not allowing gay couples to marry denies them the protection of federal benefits, which are given freely to married heterosexual couples.

That line of thinking could carry a lot of weight. In 2003, attorneys in Canada successfully argued that laws forbidding same-sex marriage went against the country's Charter of Rights and Freedoms, which is the same as the U.S. Bill of Rights. Proving that same-sex marriage bans were unconstitutional was a major turning point toward making such unions legal throughout Canada.

5 Legal Battles

All the news stories, discussions, and arguments don't mean much if they don't lead to some kind of action concerning same-sex marriage. Legalizing or banning same-sex unions—including marriage, civil unions, and domestic partnerships—are the action items that have taken place most often.

In the United States, the responsibility for same-sex marriage legislation lies primarily with state governments. However, the federal government has been persuaded, or has felt the need, to weigh in on the issue from time to time. Suddenly, same-sex marriage isn't just about who has the right to marry. The issue has also become something of a testing ground for states' rights.

Adding to the mix is the fact that gay couples also sue state governments over the right to marry. Challenging this issue in the courts is nothing new for same-sex marriage advocates. Recently, though, the number of court cases has been rising. Instead of simply asking that the state allow them to be married, gay couples and their supporters are now suing to wipe out what they see as antigay legislation.

Defense of Marriage Act

On the whole, the U.S. federal government has left the question of whether or not same-sex marriage should be legal to the states. There have been instances, however, when Congress, and even the president, have tried to influence the debate through legal means. For instance, as CNN.com reported in February 2004, then-U.S. president George W. Bush supported an amendment to the country's Constitution that would ban same-sex marriage. The measure was defeated, but it has been reintroduced several times by Congress.

Perhaps the most influential legal move by the federal government came in 1996. That is when members of Congress wrote and President Bill Clinton enacted, or put into effect, the Defense of Marriage Act. DOMA, as it is more commonly called, has two purposes. First, the law provides a federal-level definition of marriage as a "legal union between one man and one woman as husband and wife." Also, the term "spouse" is defined as "a person of the opposite sex who is a husband or a wife." Because they do not meet these legal requirements, same-sex couples are not eligible to receive the same federal benefits that are given to married heterosexuals.

The second purpose of DOMA is to ensure that states do not have to recognize one another's marriage laws. Consequently, a same-sex union may be legal in one state but not legal in others. Some gay rights groups say that this part of DOMA violates a clause in the U.S. Constitution that requires the states to respect one another's legal proceedings, including marriage. For example, if a heterosexual couple gets married in one state, they are considered legally married in every other part of the country as well. DOMA allows individual states to disrespect the legal decisions of another state with regard to same-sex marriage.

The federal Defense of Marriage Act is being used as a template for similar state laws, as protestors in Hartford, Connecticut, demonstrate by carrying signs that reference DOMA.

Those who are in favor of same-sex marriage would like to see DOMA repealed. Gay rights activists are not alone in this mission. In June 2009, President Barack Obama had signed a presidential memorandum that extended certain federal benefits to same-sex domestic partners of federal employees and civil servants. The memorandum, which acts like an executive order, not a law, also required that federal agencies comply with antidiscrimination regulations already in place.

As stated on the official White House Web site (http://www.whitehouse.gov/agenda/civil_rights), President Obama would like to repeal DOMA, as well as give same-sex couples equal federal benefits through legally recognized civil unions.

States' Rights

Even one of DOMA's creators, former U.S. representative Bob Barr of Georgia, thinks it's time to get rid of the law. In the January 5, 2009, edition of the *Los Angeles Times*, Barr states that the act "is not working out as planned" and should be scrapped. "It truly is time to get the federal government out of the marriage business," he says.

Barr's statement echoes the feelings of many across the United States who think the decision to legalize same-sex marriage should be left to the individual states. People who want the federal government to stay out of such matters do not necessarily believe that gay couples should be allowed to marry. They may simply believe in the states' right to govern marriage as they see fit.

The U.S. Constitution limits the power that the federal government has over the states. The states are guaranteed any and all rights not directly granted through the Constitution. Marriage law is one of the areas over which

"Eight" wasn't so great for same-sex couples in California as Proposition 8, banning same-sex marriage in the state, was passed in November 2008.

states have control. Supporters of same-sex marriage accuse the federal government of trying to diminish states' rights with DOMA. The U.S. government stresses that the act only applies at the federal level. States still decide who can get married within their own borders.

State Propositions and Amendments

Left to their own devices, the American states have shown disparity, or differences, regarding same-sex marriage.

Five allow same-sex marriage, and a handful offer civil unions or domestic partnerships. Many more have voted to make same-sex marriage illegal. For instance, during the 2004 elections, eleven states passed amendments to their state constitutions that made same-sex marriage illegal within their borders. Nine states proposed, or put forward, statewide bans in 2006 during state elections. Voters passed eight of those amendments or laws.

In 2008, California, Arizona, and Florida put amendments on the ballot that would make marriage between two men or two women illegal. All three passed. Probably the most talked about of these was California's Proposition 8. The California State Supreme Court had made same-sex marriage legal just a few months before the election in November. Such a quick reversal, especially in a state that is considered "gay-friendly," was surprising to many. According to the Pew Forum on Religion & Public Life, as of November 2008, a total of twenty-nine states had passed constitutional amendments making same-sex marriage illegal.

Even before California's Proposition 8 passed, same-sex marriage advocates had decided to fight fire with fire. The *Washington Post* reports that in February 2008, the Maryland General Assembly had been presented with a bill outlawing civil ceremonies for gay and hetero-sexual couples. All unions performed by the state would be called "valid domestic partnerships." Marriage would be a term reserved only for when couples were joined in a religious ceremony. As of spring 2009, the bill was still under consideration by the Maryland legislature.

Having Their Day in Court

A few legal cases regarding the right of same-sex couples to marry have appeared before state courts since the 1970s. Then in 1991, three gay couples sued the Hawaiian Department of Health for denying them marriage licenses. After five years of arguments and appeals, the Hawaiian courts ruled that denying the right to marry based on sexual orientation was against the state's constitution. Same-sex marriages should be allowed. Soon after the ruling, Hawaiians voted to add an amendment to their constitution that defines marriage as between a man and a woman only.

Despite the constitutional amendment that effectively banned same-sex marriage in the state, the court victory in Hawaii gave gay couples in the United States hope. Since then, there have been a number of trials in several states meant to decide who has the right to marry. In 2004 alone, there were at least twenty-four such cases recorded across the country. Most have been brought by multiple couples joining together. Some cases concern either the denial of marriage licenses or the granting of marital rights to a same-sex partner. Many more challenge state laws and constitutional amendments that ban same-sex marriage.

A legal suit brought by six same-sex couples was responsible for making same-sex marriage legal in California for about six months in 2008. In response, same-sex opponents passed Proposition 8. The cycle of suing continues as the California Supreme Court hears arguments regarding whether Proposition 8 is legal or merely discrimination.

Until recently, such legal battles have been fought at the state level. However, as reported in several newspapers, including the *New York Times*, activists brought suit in the federal district court in Boston in March 2009. The suit was filed on behalf of same-sex couples who had been legally married under Massachusetts law but denied federal rights and protection. The case, which is pending as of this writing, is considered to be a direct challenge to the federal Defense of Marriage Act.

Meanwhile, in Los Angeles, California, two judges in the state's federal appeals court issued orders that their employees were entitled to receive federal benefits for their same-sex partners. Court orders aren't the same as laws, however. These particular orders go against DOMA, and therefore have been ignored. The nation is waiting to see if the incident brings about more lawsuits challenging the legality of DOMA.

What the Future May Hold

6

Every time some action is taken regarding same-sex marriage, the media is full of predictions about what that action will mean in the future. One example is what happened during 2008 in California. After the state supreme court legalized same-sex marriage in May, opponents had issued warnings about what the move could mean. On the "What Is Prop 8?" Web site, opponents had stated that same-sex marriage meant schools would be forced to teach about same-sex marriage. Teaching, they had feared, would be like promoting homosexuality. The site had also claimed that freedom of religion would be attacked as religious groups could lose their tax-exempt status and be fined for preaching against same-sex marriage.

However likely or unlikely these scenarios are, the truth is no one can say for sure what will happen with same-sex marriage in the future. The best anyone can do is examine what has happened in the past and try to figure out how the public feels about the issue right now. By taking those steps, some reasonable assumptions can be made about how the same-sex debate will play out in the days to come.

Expect More Legal Challenges

In a January 2009 article in the *Advocate*, a U.S.-based gay and lesbian news magazine, legal scholar Kenji Yoshino outlined how supporters of same-sex marriage can react to state constitutional amendments such as Proposition 8. The two tactics that show the most promise are introducing a counter-amendment during the next election or taking the matter to court.

Each strategy has its pluses and minuses. Putting a pro-same-sex marriage amendment on the ballot is a legislative move. If such an amendment were to pass, opponents could not complain that gay rights activists had won by relying on the opinion of a few judges. Whether or not to add amendments is a decision made by all voters in a state. In other words, the legislative strategy would be considered more legitimate because it shows the will of the people. However, getting an amendment on the ballot, and gathering enough support to pass it, takes a lot of time and money.

Even though plans are under way to put a measure on the California ballot that would repeal Proposition 8,

As this woman's sign says, same-sex couples aren't out to ruin marriage or deny heterosexuals their rights. In many cases, all gay rights activists want is their day in court.

the matter is also being tried in the judicial system. Filing a lawsuit seems to be a quicker strategy. Elections come around only every two to four years. The American judicial system, though, guarantees citizens the right to a speedy trial. Of course, because there are lots of trials at any time, and the appeals can make the legal process take a while, "speedy" doesn't necessarily mean "immediately."

One problem with trying same-sex marriage cases in court is the risk of what's called judicial activism. Judicial activism is when new laws are instituted based on the decision of one judge or a panel of justices, instead of through public voting and elections. Laws are meant to be created by legislators, whereas judges are meant to interpret the law. Opponents of same-sex marriage worry that judges are deciding cases based on their personal beliefs, rather than the Constitution or existing laws, or are bowing to pressure from gay rights groups. In other words, there is concern that judges are not being impartial, or treating everyone equally. Proponents of same-sex marriage, though, are looking to the courts to recognize that gay people should have equal rights under the law.

Gay rights activists have been encouraged by a number of rulings that have found state bans on same-sex marriage to be discriminatory. Therefore, there probably are many more court cases regarding this issue in the United States' future.

Increased Activism

When Proposition 8 became an issue in California, each side of the same-sex marriage debate stepped up efforts to win voters over to their way of thinking. The *Los*

Angeles Times reports that more than $83 million was raised and spent by supporters and opponents of the amendment. (Opponents had a slight edge in the fund-raising race.) Pumping lots of time and money into campaigns designed to influence legislation is a trend that will probably continue for quite a long time.

Another expected development is an increase in the number of grassroots organizations that play a part in the same-sex marriage debate. Grassroots activism is a homegrown movement involving ordinary people who come together because of a shared belief that a law or policy should be changed. In a December 2008 article, the *New York Times* details the possible effect that grassroots groups may have on the future of same-sex marriage. Many of the people featured in the story had not been politically active before starting their groups. The longer the debate continues, the greater the number of people who are likely to get involved in the cause, both pro and con.

Political activism can also be as simple as voting. Backing certain political candidates and elected judges is also a way to affect future events. People generally vote for those who share their beliefs and will represent their interests. Americans can influence the future of same-sex marriage by electing the people who will create laws and decide court cases.

By exercising their right to vote and actively supporting whatever side of the gay rights debate they believe in, average citizens hold the future of same-sex couples in their hands.

The Will of the People

Although the majority of Americans do not support legalizing same-sex marriage, they do not necessarily want gay couples to be treated unfairly. When former president George W. Bush proposed a federal constitutional amendment banning same-sex marriage in 2004, an ABC News/*Washington Post* poll showed that 58 percent of Americans objected to the idea. Many members of the public seemed to be OK with the idea of civil unions and domestic partnerships that offer equal state benefits. Then as now, many folks thought gay couples should be treated fairly. They simply didn't think gay couples should be married.

Other polls and surveys show that there has been a softening in the American public's attitude toward same-sex marriage over the years. In 1999, a poll conducted by the renowned Gallup organization indicated that nearly 62 percent of the people surveyed opposed same-sex marriage. Seven years later, the same organization found that only 58 percent objected to gay couples marrying. That could signal a favorable trend for those who approve of same-sex marriage. "We can read the tea leaves," says Harvard University professor Michael Klarman in a November 2008 *U.S. News and World Report* article on Proposition 8, referring to the downward trend in opposition to gay couples marrying. "[W]e're gaining an average of 1 percent a year, so in two years, we'll fight harder and make better arguments, and we'll probably win."

Items such as Proposition 8 and the Defense of Marriage Act may eventually be repealed. If so, expect same-sex marriage opponents to create new amendments and laws that are designed as bans. Also expect same-sex marriage supporters to continue fighting any and all challenges to the rights of gay couples. In other words, as long as people, both gay and heterosexual, fall in love and wish to be married, there will be a future for this controversial issue.

Glossary

amendment An addition to a legal document.

arranged marriage When parents find a spouse for their child in a way that's kind of like a business agreement.

civil union A legal agreement designed to recognize the commitment of gay couples under the law.

clergy Religious leaders and workers who perform rites, such as marriages.

controversy An event or concept about which people have differing opinions.

discrimination Treating people unfairly based on class, religion, race, or sexual orientation.

domestic partnership A legal relationship that is similar to a civil union, only with fewer benefits.

dowry A gift of money and goods that a bride's family gives to the groom.

grassroots Basic or fundamental; grassroots political movements start with small, basic groups of ordinary people.

judicial activism Social change that is brought about by judicial decree; the doctrine that the judicial branch, especially the federal courts, may interpret the U.S. Constitution by deviating from legal precedent (established custom or practice) as a means of bringing about legal and social change.

legislation The making of laws.

levirate The practice of marrying a brother's widow to keep family bloodlines intact.

matrimony The state of being married.

morality The ability to tell the difference between right and wrong, and choosing to do the right thing.

polygamy Having more than one spouse at a time.

prenuptial Occurring or existing before a marriage.

proposition A legal plan that is decided by a popular vote.

repeal To cancel; to officially end the validity of something such as a law.

scriptures The holy, sacred writings of different world religions.

slippery slope A situation that starts a bad chain of events.

states' rights Rights guaranteed to individual states under the U.S. Constitution; concerning a balance of power between state and federal governments.

theologian An expert in theology, or the study of the nature of God and religious belief.

For More Information

Alliance Defense Fund

15100 North Ninetieth Street

Scottsdale, AZ 85260

(800) TELL-ADF (834-4233)

Web site: http://www.alliancedefensefund.org/
     main/defult.aspx

The Alliance Defense Fund is a legal alliance defending religious freedom through strategy, training, funding, and litigation.

Canadian Lesbian and Gay Archives

50 Charles Street East

Toronto, ON M4Y 2N6

Canada

(416) 777-2755

Web site: http://www.clga.ca

The CLGA collects and maintains information related to gay and lesbian life in Canada and elsewhere. The organization makes its books and articles, artifacts, audio and video recordings, and artwork available to the public for education and research.

Egale Canada

310-396 Cooper Street

Ottawa, ON K2P 2H7

Canada

(613) 230-1043

Web site: http://www.egale.ca
Egale Canada advances equality and justice for lesbian, gay, bisexual, and transgender people and their families across Canada.

Family Research Council

801 G Street NW

Washington, DC 20001

(800) 225-4008

Web site: http://www.frc.org
Founded in 1983, the Family Research Council is "dedicated to the promotion of marriage, family, and the sanctity of human life in national policy. Through books, pamphlets, media appearances, public events, debates, and testimony, FRC's team of experienced policy experts review data and analyze proposals that impact family law and policy" in the United States.

Gay & Lesbian Alliance Against Defamation—East Coast

104 West 29th Street, Fourth Floor

New York, NY 10001

(212) 629-3322

Web site: http://www.glaad.org
The Gay & Lesbian Alliance Against Defamation promotes fair and inclusive representation in the media as a way to eliminate discrimination based on gender identity and sexual orientation.

Gay & Lesbian Alliance Against Defamation—West Coast

5455 Wilshire Boulevard, #1500

Los Angeles, CA 90036

(323) 933-2240

Lambda Legal

120 Wall Street, Suite 1500

New York, NY 10005-3904

(212) 809-8585

Web site: http://www.lambdalegal.org

Lambda Legal is a "national organization committed to achieving full recognition of the civil rights of lesbians, gay men, bisexuals, transgender people, and those with HIV through impact litigation, education, and public policy work."

National Gay and Lesbian Task Force

1325 Massachusetts Avenue NW, Suite 600

Washington, DC 20005

(202) 393-5177

Web site: http://www.thetaskforce.org

With several chapters across the United States, the National Gay and Lesbian Task Force promotes pro-gay legislation, and provides research and policy analysis.

Web Sites

Due to the changing nature of Internet links, Rosen Publishing has developed an online list of Web sites related to the subject of this book. This site is updated regularly. Please use this link to access this list:

http://www.rosenlinks.com/itn/marr

For Further Reading

Andryszewski, Tricia. *Same-Sex Marriage: Moral Wrong or Civil Right?* Minneapolis, MN: Twenty-First Century Books, 2008.

Chauncey, George. *Why Marriage? The History Shaping Today's Debate Over Gay Equality*. Cambridge, MA: Basic Books, 2004.

Friedman, Lauri S. *Introducing Issues with Opposing Viewpoints—Gay Marriage*. Westport, CT: Greenwood Press, 2005.

Hudson, David L., Jr. *Gay Rights* (Point/Counterpoint). New York, NY: Chelsea House Publishers, 2005.

Kafka, Tina. *Gay Rights*. Farmington Hills, MI: Lucent Books, 2006.

Moats, David. *Civil Wars: The Battle for Gay Marriage*. Fort Washington, PA: Harvest Books, 2005.

Sobel, Syl. *The Bill of Rights: Protecting Our Freedom Then and Now*. Hauppauge, NY: Barrons Educational Series, 2008.

Stefoff, Rebecca. *Marriage* (Open for Debate). Salt Lake City, UT: Benchmark Books, 2006.

Walzer, Lee. *Gay Rights on Trial: A Handbook with Cases, Laws, and Documents*. Indianapolis, IN: Hackett Publishing Company, 2004.

Bibliography

Andryszewski, Tricia. *Same-Sex Marriage: Moral Wrong or Civil Right?* Minneapolis, MN: Twenty-First Century Books, 2008.

BBC News. "Gay Marriage Around the Globe." December 2005. Retrieved March 12, 2009 (http://news.bbc.co.uk/2/hi/americas/4081999.stm).

CBS News. "CBS Poll: Changing Views on Gay Marriage." July 2008. Retrieved March 12, 2009 (http://www.cbsnews.com/stories/2008/06/13/opinion/polls/main4180335.shtml).

Ewers, Justin. "As Connecticut Allows Same-Sex Marriage, the Debate Continues in California." *U.S. News and World Report*, November 13, 2008. Retrieved March 8, 2009 (http://www.usnews.com/articles/news/national/2008/11/13/as-connecticut-allows-same-sex-marriage-the-debate-continues-in-california.html).

Gay & Lesbian Alliance Against Defamation. "In Focus: Public Opinion and Polls." *Media Reference Guide.* Retrieved March 19, 2009 (http://www.glaad.org/media/guide/infocus/polls.php).

Goodnough, Abby, and Katie Zezima. "Suit Seeks to Force Government to Extend Benefits to Same-Sex Couples." *New York Times*, March 2, 2009. Retrieved March 19,

2009 (http:///www.nytimes.com/2009/03/03/us/ 03marriage.html?ref=us).

Knapp, Alex. "The Universal Idea of Marriage (or Lack Thereof)." *Heretical Ideas*, August 2008. Retrieved January 28, 2009 (http://www.hereticalideas.com/2008/ 08/the-universal-idea-of-marriage-or-lack-thereof).

McKinley, Jesse. "Gay Marriage Ban Inspires New Wave of Activists." *New York Times*, December 9, 2008, p. 23.

Miller, Lisa. "The Religious Argument for Gay Marriage." *Newsweek*, Vol. CLII, No. 24, December 15, 2008, pp. 28–31.

Mitchell, Linda Elizabeth. *Family Life in the Middle Ages*. Westport, CT: Greenwood Publishing Group, 2007.

Moore, Maloy. "Proposition 8. Tracking the Money: Final Numbers." *Los Angeles Times*, February 3, 2009. Retrieved March 19, 2009 (http://www.latimes.com/news/ local/politics/cal/la-moneymap,0,5374284.htmlstory).

Morris, David, and Gary Langer. "Same-Sex Marriage: Most Oppose It, but Balk at Amending the Constitution." ABCNews.com, 2004. Retrieved March 19, 2009 (http://abcnews.go.com/sections/us/ Relationships/same_sex_marriage_poll_040121.html).

Nelson, Christine. "Civil Unions and Domestic Partnership Statutes." National Conference of State Legislatures, March 2008. Retrieved March 28, 2009 (http://www.ncsl.org/programs/cyf/civilunions_dome sticpartnership_statutes.htm).

New York Times. "No Separate but Equal in Marriage." April 1, 2007. Retrieved March 10, 2009 (http://www. nytimes.com/2007/04/01/opinion/nyregionopinions/ CTgay.html).

Pawelski, James G., et. al. "The Effects of Marriage, Civil Union, and Domestic Partnership Laws on the Health and Well-Being of Children." *Pediatrics*, Vol. 118, No. 1, July 2006, pp. 349–364.

Pew Forum on Religion & Public Life. "States with Voter-Approved Constitutional Bans on Same-Sex Marriage, 1998–2008." November 13, 2008. Retrieved April 3, 2009 (http://pewforum.org/docs/?DocID=370).

Rein, Lisa. "Bill Would End Civil Marriage, Create Domestic Partnerships." *Washington Post*, February 5, 2008, p. B04.

Romero, Adam P., et. al. "Census Snapshot: The United States (Census Snapshots)." Williams Institute, UCLA School of Law, December 2007, p. 1. Retrieved March 12, 2009 (http://www.law.ucla.edu/williamsinstitute/ publications/USCensusSnapshot.pdf).

Wilson, Scott. "President Wades into Gay Issues: Order Gives Some Benefits to Partners of Federal Workers." *Washington Post*, June 18, 2009. Retrieved June 18, 2009 (http://www.washingtonpost.com/wp-dyn/ content/article/2009/06/17/AR2009061702578.html).

Yoshino, Kenji. "Prop.8: Which Way Now?" Advocate.com, January 13, 2009. Retrieved March 19, 2009 (http:// www.advocate.com/issue_story_ektid67115.asp).

Index

About the Author

Jeanne Nagle is a journalist and author from upstate New York. She has conducted extensive research on issues involving gay rights, the fruits of which labor are included in this book. Among other titles Nagle has written for Rosen Publishing is *GLBT Teens and Society* (Teens: Being Gay, Lesbian, Bisexual, or Transgender).

Photo Credits

Cover (top, left) Scott Olson/Getty Images; cover (top, right) Shutterstock.com; cover (bottom), pp. 4, 7 David Paul Morris/Getty Images; pp. 5, 11, 21, 34, 41, 47, 49 © AP Images; pp. 14, 18 Thomas & Joanna Ainscough/Wikipedia; p. 16 © Museumslandschaft Hessen Kassel Ute Brunzel/Bridgeman Art Library; pp. 23, 25 Alden Pellett/Getty Images; p. 27 Tim Boyle/Getty Images; p. 28 © Jack Krutz/ZUMA Press; pp. 30, 37 Mark Ralston/AFP/Getty Images; p. 32 Amanda Edwards/Getty Images; pp. 39, 43 © Robert Galbraith/Reuters/Landov; p. 52 © Margot Duane/ZUMA Press.

Designer: Tom Forget; Editor: Kathy Kuhtz Campbell;
Photo Researcher: Amy Feinberg